TREE HERESIES

MERCER
UNIVERSITY PRESS

Endowed by
TOM WATSON BROWN
and
THE WATSON-BROWN FOUNDATION, INC.

TREE HERESIES

Poems

William Wright

MERCER UNIVERSITY PRESS | Macon, Georgia

MUP/ P501

Published by Mercer University Press
1501 Mercer University Drive
Macon, Georgia 31207

9 8 7 6 5 4 3 2 1

Books published by Mercer University Press are printed on acid-free paper that meets the requirements of the American National Standard for Information Sciences—Permanence of Paper for Printed Library Materials.
ISBN 978-0-88146-520-4
Cataloging-in-Publication Data is available from the Library of Congress

for my parents, sister, and Michelle

Contents

Acknowledgments

I would like to thank The Morris Museum of Art for awarding "Prologue" and "Aubade for Yellow Jacket" the first and second prizes for the Porter Fleming Award in Poetry. With thanks, too, to Dan Corrie, for his generosity and his encouragement. And with incalculable love for Michelle, who's sacrificed so much.

Asheville Poetry Review: "Boyhood Trapped behind the Eyelids," "Jack, Snake-bitten, 1937"
Atlanta Review: "Flowers in a Northern Field," "Tree Heresies," "Something New and Moonburnt"
Birmingham Poetry Review: "Sleep" (a section of "Inflorescence")
Broad River Review: "Nocturne for Cicada"
Cimarron Review: "Sleeping Underground"
Connecticut Review: "The Farmer Who Loved Winter"
Flycatcher: A Journal of Native Imagination: "Shawnee Trail"
Louisiana Literature: "Ghosts in Winter," "Nightfall"
New South: "Salt Marsh"
Poetry South: "Question," "Silence"
Rattle: "Nightmare, Revised"
Shenandoah: "Barn Gothic," "First Day in October," "My Other Body" (as "Nora")
Southern Poetry Review: "A Path through Walnut Trees after Rain," "A Study of Descent"
Tar River Poetry: "Aubade for Yellow Jacket"
Terrain.org: "June's Account," "Tincture," "Furnace and Fox"
The Texas Review: "The Milk Witch," "Run-off," "History of the Last Man"
Waccamaw: "The Book of Nights"
Xavier Review: "Eight Essays on a North Carolina Farm, 1920."

I. For the Insomniac Plagued by Thoughts of Time

Prologue

1.

You have taken a road into a place you do not know—
off the green cusp of mountains, or up from sandstung
marshes, you are here and you are

here: Down piedmont dusks where soils
meld from loam to clay to dust and back to loam,
a wavering pedosphere, home to plum and scuppernong

over which bats fling themselves blind, demon-toothed
through barn lofts and lamplight, over silos and water towers
and miles-off county roads where stars now rise.

Where sparrows make houses of ruined chimneys
and storms roar from cumulonimbi, gourds
poured by phantom giants to set peach trees steaming,

caught between here and the other world. Where foxes
scream the woods to sacredness,
and owls crouch the limbs spirit-eyed to watch

for mouse-skitter or skink. In creeks red minnows gather
in still pools, each spine lumbered for the moment's purpose.
Water moccasins drag the black fires of their bodies

into sandstone fractures, their torsional smolder
unseen. Wind bends east through thicker flora,
and gangs of mange-pocked dogs lope and skulk

in their lusts and through low woods fireflies constellate
sumac and bamboo. Below, milk caps and devil's
urn sprout alien, clustered. Leaves open: east-most fields fallow

with neglect. A swamp stagnates, impaled with a derelict
truck, mattresses, a charred tractor and heaps of cattle bones.
Hundreds of glass bottles, jars. Moldering rats. Trash-richness

growing shoreward, piling up grass banks gone toxic,
only to collapse again into this smutty stew.
Surface's oil haze, prismatic. No life in this water.

Near these earthen cancers a high shed with music, coarse
laughter where farmhands gather to myth out their emptiness
in tequila and *cervesas*, lewd jokes. Their faces are soot-smeared,

sunbrowned, smiling raucous, muscled, their eyes half-mast
and brains staved pattern and drone. For what can the heart
carry from this place? And what is home but the distant

windowdark where thin flowers sprout from the single
sill's empty can? Crucifix pollinated in nicotine.
Yards where grass will not grow, where women break

yearly and yearly until nights drain dreamless
toward their husbands' pre-dawn orders. Trucks huff
morning's swelter. To rehearse the orchard

into mass, leave it bone.

2.

Townward, field's edges matted in leaf-litter decades old, clogged
in the pox of sweet gum saplings and glass.
An earth left igneous, ignored.

This land flat save the sheer knolls of creeks
flushed with summer storm, heliophilic
silences that drain into copse creeks.

Pervading smells of sawdust, iron, gasoline. Maws of
private wells, groundwater moon-doused. Fields
shunted upwind with train howls, window rattlers

forcing in slumbering country brains dreams
of churches burning, the ax chopped wrong to hack
blood from body, hex and freak of late April frost.

Ghost-choked country. Where no ear
stops for story, lest metaphor siphons bible tongue,
lest image shake loose weathers to kill the seed.

3.

One church in town, caustic architecture, white
and sheer, the steeple rusting starward. Orthogonal
spectral force to town streets and dark therein.

Shops of snuff, tobacco, little candy tins, pipes,
knives and nails, the smells of metal, oil,
and sweetness so rich they dizzy passersby.

Now the clerks exit their back doors, tired,
retreat from wares into brick alleyways,
into structured dark, somewhere they call home.

County's south where new roads untether the horse
forever, the asphalt's bitumen, exhaust and rubber smells
confluenced with rotten peaches, skunk,

the flower stench of walnuts, carried clear and pure
to the county's north tip. Here, a phalanx of older trees,
tall and conspiratorial, panoptic, swaying.

A backroad twines to a gravel driveway flanked by poplars, coils
serpentine for a quarter mile up to a brown Victorian house,
large porch with swing and hydrangea hugging

the perimeter. Inside, immaculate sadness:
china and silver behind glass, a polished dining room
table set for two but never used, all beds bed-skirted

and the attic spiderless. Cellar jar-clogged
with jellies and beans to keep years. So clean
a patch of dust strikes the eye almost sexual.

Kitchen floor lit in squares of failing light, and on
the counter a saucer of butter softening. No one
here, no sound save the ticking of joists and ceiling

corners. Old sepia pictures of frowning forebears
mid-field, or family portraits, hardships rendered
in furrowed brows, hard-bled flesh and land.

4.

Upstairs, she turns in her pain. Smells
of soap and tea, smells of her hair strung
white with sweat, harrowed sleep.

Bedsprings groan. Her long breath. Wordless
and still, supine, eyes cordoned off from joy.
The house cold with dark, even as behind it

now the falling sun gloams blood-red over
this patch of orchard saved for blood kin—
these fragile trees sugaring night-wind.

5.

Here he walks, slow, lumbering, drunk
on day's vestige heat, cloud's downslant
through tree-line, the distances of far-off towns.

To stand this ground now and tame
days to peaches, profit, to lift, till and spray,
to help his hands cull back the days.

To stay here till deepest twilight, boots still on loam,
leaning faint and moonburnt into what he cannot change.
Glances back houseward to the high window,

lamp snuffed, knows she stares dead-eyed at nothing,
a nun to her lost son, to the snapped umbilicus
of years where memory is water and his end.

From that day on, the moon to her: an ossified eye.
From that day on, any gladness in him
algebraic or underling to the unmovable:

the near woods' creek-flow and oxbow silicates,
deep arrowpoints long buried, lodged for millennia:
clovis, bannerstone, half-dimes, and knapped chert.

Hidden narratives of creekside mothers, onyx-haired,
laughter and bowls boiling with hunted meat.
Clothed in deerskin, turtle shell rattles for the green

corn dance. Villages gathered at rivers to fish
and feed over fires beneath vegetal gods.
Now only stone: Quartz, schist, silt.

English pipes. Beads and awls, novaculite drills,
pottery shards, flint scrawls and scraps stitched
through remnants of animal and human alike,

stone-ghosted testimony in underground layers no human
shall see again. Still downward, Pleistocene imprints,
amuleted dents of moon-old gestures, cruxed

in bivalves and bryozoans, earth of Pangaea
before stromatolites and Hadean protohistory, magma fire
and comet, dust and this turning galactic allusion.

Aubade for Yellow Jacket

Dawn light sets them smoldering,
tiny gold-black fires that scorch the yard's
heart. They pulse: in, out, in, out

of a mud-ringed tear, where their crazed
focus seeks wood-pulp for nested tiers.
Guards click, seethe for queen and brood.

Something hums under this hill,
an open mouth that sucks the searing
sugars every August drips. Something

chews earth to paper dust and builds
these buried cells well into day's end,
when most dusks fail to douse

summer-stubborn heat. Grass crackles:
such a drone, a throb of anger here.
Hard to hate them for this madness

to outdo what will do them in, as fall
bleeds queens to flakes and new kin
hatch, winter-hidden, waiting.

Nocturne for Cicada

Down where the pines scuff the moon,
they rattle the woods to whir and static,
scrims of sound, vatic music so loud

at times it lodges in the ear like a burr,
carries through sleep a soundtrack
of farmhouses under stars, the slant

land's windfall leaves they settle in to scar.
Red-eyed dusk-chisels: they whittle the mind
so sharp it conjures collapsing ice

on a pond at winter's bladed end,
a crack in the attic window. Fork tines
clicking on a clean plate. The miracle of a silver

pocket-watch unclasped and ticking still
after years locked in a cedar box. To scrape
and sing the sun down, swell poplar

and elm through wind and wind time
back to earth's first songs. To play
that instrument, counterpoint the night.

Barn Gothic

Red as a cardinal, it leans ruined in winter's gray field,
form falling against a sycamore,
its older, wiser wife.

Closer in, a fox den
in the hay tunnel light where green eyes haunt
the nearby mountain woods and stars cast

silver glyphs on the rotting floor:
Rain has felled the structure's roof.
Here horses pitched and leaned

into chaff, awaiting work,
this room still alive in smells of oil, dung,
and cedar-heart. Swallows twig

warped boards, black widows
float, wait
in corners to wrap and gore what passes.

Wasps caulk the loft's cracked seams,
and mice hide from owls, eyes,
their lives the barn's heart

beating behind the walls.

Horsemint scent finds
the barn's chinks. Moonflower
grips, twines

the rusted scythe and the burled
yawn of the caved-in door: Earth
                    sculpts without consent,

remnants hallowed, restored—
Autumns, when the air shucks
                    rain to hollow starriness,

the moon strikes the barn just right:
White moths hoard here where lanterns
                    have long been snuffed,

where the only fires are the moths themselves,
their flock come to love this place and perhaps
                    the stars, too, all pure, radiant, dying.

Nightmare, Revised

Now it is not a man pinned eviscerated
to a barn door and stretched mothlike
to show his brisket,

the drying jewels of his viscera
and his teeth red-tinged, eyes
scappled bald. Now it is

not a plum-colored sky over
foothills of ruined chimneys,
the world forever October.

Instead, I stand in a field where there is no
barn, and the pinned man, my father,
has been let down, sewn back to life:

He walks through his home, his loneliness
a dark carapace. His mother lies
in a pine box in a South Carolina

graveyard. By now her eyes are fused
and sunken. By now her mouth is
a leather smudge. She wanted cremation

but the family would not have it.
The bones of her fingers poke through skin—
The moon impales the night.

The smell of smoke blooms on the sweet-sharp air,
and I feel a joy under the thin arbor
of passing clouds.

I feel a joy, because there is no secret order
of moth or plum, chimney
or bone, only the pungent fact

that somewhere, somewhere beyond my sight,
a fire burns part of this
land gone, gone.

Boyhood Trapped Behind the Eyelids

We knew nothing that summer
        summoned the grasses and stars,
                were maps for our skin as we ran

through leaf-litter, the sweet juice
        of scuppernongs sugaring our throats
                and fat hornets in their paper

nests hanging like scorched cauls
        and through the night-woods where
                we broke into the skitter of goat bones—

The ancient man from Africa whose visage
        pruned through the windy leaves
                in the dull lamplight—and how we dreamed

of the olive complexion of the older girl's
        breasts she'd let us see one day in the
                loft, and even a flash of the peach-fuzz

cleft behind her panties so that nights
        I ached and tried to will her candor
                beside me, over me, under me, her

breath hot in my eyes and her cheeks
        flecked in olive freckles. And into fall
                when the ridge of peach trees swelled

into a galaxy of red-pink planets, we took
        to orchards and made forts to hide
                and witness with a child's fear

migrants weave and yell in truckbeds
treading the clay rows. And October's swollen
twilights folded us into the unspoken

knowledge that our blood was our fathers'—
our blood pulsed our shapes
into the sculpture of our kin, when

winter took over and the snowdrifts skinned
the sky of its blue muscle to render
the bone-whiteness of full cold,

forced us into the heat of ovens and mothers to watch
the blur of each other in the gauzed glass of windows next
door, to wait again for springmelt's warm throb.

My Other Body

—in memory of Patricia Highsmith's "Oona"

My other body, the body
that has forgotten me, stood up
one day out in the country

that has never been my home
(he chopped his own kindling
and tended a ridge of apple trees)

and walked through the chicory
stubble, the blue glow of hidden
things molded by every fall,

and left his wife. When she smiled,
her mouth was like a squat fork lacking
the two central tines, a gap

in her upper teeth that gave
her family's misery away.
Woman of fraught days, dying fields.

She wrapped her hair in a dry,
coppery bun. Soon, the other men
of that country, who had watched her

for a long time, moved in on her,
for they had always detected something
sensual in the way she threshed

the grass, her stare sharp, locked,
a look that told them her heart
was wan with indifference, compliance.

They heard her say in dreams they never
remembered: *Come and touch*
the dark spaces, come and stave

my grief for which there is no cure.
One man fixed her rusted well,
one built her a gambrel barn,

and still another bought
her the best shoat he could find
in three counties. A few brought

flowers, candy, tins of sweetbread.
Soon they offered nothing,
for she smiled at them all the same, let them

stick their tongues and fingers
in that hollow gap without the least
resistance. Her belly never grew,

though gossip swelled, churned,
as gossip will: Even the old men,
mostly silent, gathered

to gum their tobacco on
moth-freighted porches at nightfall
to tell what they had heard,

scandal igniting the long-dim heartwood
of their minds. The other women
of that country, growing

bitter, hateful, spat her name,
snarled at the far meadow
where she bent with work.

Hated the ease with which their men slid
into her exhaustion, the ease
with which she stitched the days together.

Nights, these women did not
dream of my other self in their loneliness,
how he stopped to witness

the wild furnaces of moonflowers
burn, to catch the stretched, pineal heads
of poplars grow heavy and bowed

with storm. How the seams
between branches revealed
nothing save distant fires that gave

no light. That he went on, away from
that country, withdrew into dark
between the white, laughing leaves.

Sleeping Underground

My earthen mask is wet with weeks of rain.
Slaked roots stretch, drowsy in a cave of loam.
Smells: deer, toad, worm, pepperbush, and hazel
pervade my constant dream of stars, the dusty ice

of comets. On my side I dream of cities, the dun fog
that haunts those scalded roads. On my back, I recall
grandfather's hawklike eyes. Face down, I'm blinded
with visions of fallow fields, scorched leaves

on a sluggish river. No matter: I'd rather be here,
close to cattle bones, broken cauldrons, rags and scraps
slaves threw away, hymns that still thrum through this hill—
remnants of their hush harbors—torch sticks, night gowns,

and bibles gone to dust. If I could twine my sleep to history,
memory to nerve and pulse, I could sit up in this dark, disturb
the land to recall shreds of those songs, the warm
resolve in words, reprieves from death's avian stare.

Tree Heresies

Even as the dream begins, the light a lemon
yellow through the window, even as the vision
of the woods breaking into impossibly green
flames grind the sleeping heart to utterance,

I cannot tell you what the dream means.
And even as this song roots into the ear
and routes the childhood songs the mind
has latched to for years and years, trust this

music to destroy the freight of definitions,
this hex of words guarding the central dark.
Heat rises and wavers; grass wilts
into the worms, but all is not as it has always been—

weeks scuttle by like sun-speared
centipedes—trees and houses fade through
their motions, lamps click off—
Gravity and memory relume the pulse

for something closer to the burgeoning leaf,
for something nearer the necessary fires
that kept our ancient dead gathered
around that bloody, beautiful fear.

June's Account

—After Steve Brown and for Dan Corrie

In this, the sixth month, birds insist
the morning to a jarring bliss—but to think
of the cold blossoming from a sparrow's

breath in winter's stone stillness
is to find these sonatas mockery, mantic
surrenders to summer's scald.

Behind these days of flecked glass and tea,
the potted spill of fern and phlox,
from these hours of leafhurt, these galaxies

of scattered grass, something speaks
beneath the earth—not devil or creature
or even bone, but sepulchered memory,

sounds star-silent, annulled of tongue,
no less language to tabulate
this algebraic bloom and bough.

Something New and Moonburnt

It'll have to be a valley of thriving
timber where women make soap
and men fill jars with tadpoles

and sons break from their
angsts not with blood
but with fistfuls of jonquils

or bloodroot. Daughters
will drive the horses away
from the yolklight of cookfires.

Night, night. Night will be
the new day and the families
will sit beneath the planets

and torn flesh will be stitched,
bread broken, and the new
violence an acquiescence

to the notion that nothing
need be carried, no more
than the body can bear.

Lantern Sparrow

When the shadow of sleet fell across the bed,
I entered a sadness I had never felt before,
where sparrows flew through snowfall to find

the white scrabble of my yard and the house's
charred remains still smoldered. A lone flue
stood gnarled, half-collapsed. One sparrow landed

there on the blackened brick, preened as snow
fell runic and skewed in the dusk while the quarrel
of its kind, the hundreds it had come with,

bannered away through cedardark, the frigid,
moonless air. Its gray-brown dullness seemed
to bend the winter stars down

the gray-brown distance—until at once
its heart and tiny brisket glowed from within,
the garnet lungs and ruby heart. Lantern-sparrow,

ghost-sparrow, sparrow of country roads gone
to the snowlight of spilled milk. Bird-of-ember,
bird-of-ruin that made me love the beauty,

the austere purity of that fragility. Had I
that sparrow, I would call it kin, have it sleep
in a tiny basket of grass at my feet, let it haunt

the attic's beams and rafters. If the sparrow
were mine, I would ask it nothing about the night,
only savor its clarity, its warmth in my hands.

Shawnee Trail

Near the creepweed, a road-kill hare, the head
fully detached from the rotten torso,
the ribs shattered, browned in sun.

No vulture, no alms. The trees stand still
as graves, dark smudges on the gauze
of afternoon. The sun, a blinded eye.

Soon, the moth-light of evening, when gullies
shine, ditches of pentecost until full dark,
when a single firefly coils like a ghost seed

down the dusk's throat. Moments lost
in death and beauty, death and beauty.
Fine: Let summer break its back again

on hidden stones, the wilted leaves,
the trillion vines that search the dark
for something to clutch and conquer.

Attic and Image

When the attic door collapsed from the ceiling,
we looked up into that rectangular dark and smelled
the musk of years weep down into the lit spaces

where we walk and speak and sleep and eat. Dusts
of moldering apples and a blue-stained wedding veil,
a throng of larvae that hatched and flew

from a wayward cowbird who happened, one
frigid December, into a darkness not its own.
And in all that still haunts us from this dull heaven,

the day's vestige heat, the musk of storm-fraught
rafters that bend and warp in perfect anonymity,
the bony profile of that bird, kept in the dark bird-shaped stamp

of dust on the curved sill of the attic window
that I have not seen but know is there,
that bird-shape blasted by the sun and haunted

by stars for decades in this normal house on a normal street
with its normal consent to gravity,
that image is what I take with me now to sleep.

First Day of October

A gray leaf enshrouds the earth.
I think of how rain shifts eastward
into Carolina, how the clouds siphon highways

of any least shadow. Where is my father but on the moss-
ridden hill of his yard, the leaves still clinging
to summer's last pulse? Where is my mother

but caught in her panic, the foothills
of north Georgia crashing into each other
with a slowness that belies the season's contrition,

to destroy the green summer always commands?
Beneath us, the earth roils; smoke plumes
from sea-depths where soft, pale creatures,

forever severed of color and light, click, stumble
to find something, anything in their blindness.

Tincture

First wood smoke scent on the wind—
        lungs twinned full of fire's sharpness,
charwood ghosting down through a northeast
        growing colder. Land of chimneys

and bibles. When all creatures begin
        their hidden dens, when mornings spin clearer
and the moon scythes through day's blue harvest—
        One star dies there, remnant mineral

that shimmers and unshackles fall's fluency,
        unwinds the body into trestle and scar.
Not honesty, but clarity that mothers the eyes
        into the dimming, imperishable pasture.

Furnace and Fox

1.

Tonight so clear the Milky Way shimmers like a stoked furnace,
the scattered stars like rogue embers deep in a bloomery.

I recall my father's face, the orange light of the wood stove
imprisoned in his skin, his eyes trapping the firelight

until he'd lobbed and poked the pine logs, then shut
and latched the grate. The chimney roiled the wind

with the sweet-sharp scent of charred trees, a smell
that I catch tonight through the open window despite

the lingering scent of a cold rain that's come and gone,
rushed and vanished over town like smoke.

2.

That was the year my father smelled of tobacco and rum,
leather and stone, the year the house creaked hollow,

ticking down into the gravity of his loneliness. That was the year
his silence began in earnest, the months he embraced

his bitterness, mantled it on his body like a second skin.
Nothing mattered then save the language of the woods—

the single plum tree sprouting tiny, sour hearts, the bullfrogs'
blaring counterpoint to owls that never asked any question,

only swooped to snag a shrew or mouse and disappear
into the darkness of their hunger. That winter, the nights

were stitched with screams, half-human, half-angel, nephilim
wails that braided through trees so loud they woke one

from deepest dreams of attics afire, of possession lost to the throat
of flame. They woke one to stand dizzy and stumble numb-footed

out into the cold with no malice, only dazed wonder at the face
that glowed low from the dead leaves: a fox so still and obsessed

it became a creature of ruby, of snow-mask and bloodroot—
a creature whose radiance granted my father rare joy, first healing.

In Fear of Silence

Tonight, in pain, I lean into the blueness
of dusk after reading poems to a crowd:
No one follows me into the ground-
lit corridors of western

South Carolina, where pines jag the moon's
belly, and orchards kneel under stars.
No one can hope to understand
these fields' rapt emptiness.

Once, I saw a man walk far-off in the faint
glow of a street lamp just off the north tip
of Yonce's packing shed. He had clearly
lost his mind. Even at that

distance, I could hear him barking at twilight,
screaming *You goddamned better give me
back my mouth*. He vanished in high
weeds and I heard what Christ

allows: the truck engines of teenagers murderous
with boredom, bullfrogs, the human screams
of rabbits dying in their dens. The houses
ticking gaunt and lean, long and crumbling

in the fullness of every season—silence here
the one necessity, the one stone that freights
every tongue lest someone dare suggest silence
and silence only beyond the sun.

Hour

If I walk the sun-killed grass
among the farmlight of summer
mornings where I know

my footsteps alter forever
the shape, the geometry
of this earth;

if I step through gray stones
of old rail yards at night
when one blue star

claims the seam winter pines allow;
if I move through evening's
blood-stained hours

and the briars scrape, drag some
of me with them into roots;
if I consider old men

stare through their memories on skewed
porches across these fields—
the dimmed weathers

of their minds grown colder,
the woodpiles of their years
now cindered cauls—

and if I admit the world is
kind, even as it murders
my cells and days,

even as it kills, sculpts my joys
into a hidden box of bone,
dust, and worm,

my heart blooms orchard-deep
to know this earth has made for me
an hour of seasons, seeds,

and sentience, for which I am
nun, priest, imam: married
to all it withholds.

One Third of Our Lives

Tell me sleep strikes, coils, vanishes
like a serpent made of smoke
leaving nothing of itself

but lidless eyes. Tell me the night recites
its own story, and let it be a narrative
of burning, of bloom,

of goats that bend to clover, then rise
to translate stars to grammar
only slatted pupils

parse. Someone has doused
himself in gasoline
and lit a match,

and the crackling ceiling of his shack
caves in on him: the sashes
bulge; windows

shatter, smoke: We sleep on,
smiling as a phantom moth
alights upon our hair.

We sleep as starlings shunt down
nightfall like thrown stones
and land in western fields

where sun still flares leaning
trees to flame. Just outside
these windows, a woman

stands and watches the sole
lamplit room for a moving
shadow. A spider sits

on her hand, witness.
Every headlight that paints
the walls to dappled calculus

is ghost, so tell me that sleep
is more than these nightly
wombs of blue

narcosis, more than our mouths
slackening, rehearsing
early for the dust.

Summer Insomnia

Night corpulent with clouds
and thunderless lightning, heat
mirrored in the weed-eaten yard,

held hostage by the house
whose attic sags, wolf-wool insulation
baking down to dust.

Not the ticks and pops of winter,
but a swollen groan, a plan
to warp and weep wood rotten.

How to sleep in such stagnancy?
Ten fans spin the rooms to loud
breathing, but the earth hurtles

in utter silence toward the violent
grammars of a new day, the east
turning back again to glare.

The Book of Nights

Again, wind drags the alphabet of nothing
and everything through bent trees, leaves
that utter promises already broken,

half-heard whispers that seize the dark
threads of sleep from my eyes with surgical
care. The body's warmth is

the body's assent to drowning,
its consent to winter.
And yet summer's green gears

grind the heart to such friction that it scalds,
it sears the center: The clock's hands burn
and I turn to face the wall.

Far away, a girl in a rust-crazed city laughs
toward madness, plucking strands of her hair
from her scalp, one by one, dark red

hair she's combed a thousand times
into a garnet veil. Something had changed
her brain to foxfire, something has

placed a dull green light in her mouth.
When she finally sleeps, her hands rest, puritanical,
prophetic, across her chest. We share nothing

save a steady unraveling, the ways
things are siphoned by ditches and stars,
rain and salt, wrenched away by force

of rivers and blossoms to the source of any
small loss where a little, just a little
truth leaks through.

II. Inflorescence

Salt Marsh

The smell hits like egg and a lemon
left out too long. Brackish light stings

the eyes: a billion eyes stare back
from halophytic shrubs, crouch-blossomed,

furtive in their windless days. The world's
beginning, end: deltaic, estuarine,

back-barrier, open coast, embayment
or drowned lowland, houses

of living carpets, blue-green algal blooms
that bind to themselves silt, salt—

sea lavender, sedge and rush.
Where cordgrass and glasswort line

mudflats, roots shooting
through substrate to summon more.

Flowers in a Northern Field

The heart draws to what it does
not know: Not arctic, but north
enough for purple saxifrage
to grow: Perhaps near Halifax
in autumn, when trillium or trout
lilies wilt in upper meadows,
and rime climbs the loosestrife
spikes until they bow and crack:
north, a mythic north, where
baneberry and blue-eyed grass
flux gorges through a colder
country, where crux and mind
can witness, gather, come home
to warm beside the glowing pine.

Run-off

Rain puddle's
mica shimmer
under the sluice-
drain, star-fleck
surrogate, caesura
for the shuttered eye.
Implicative, froth
of storm-scar, scum:
Opalescent dark
sparring light—
No source
for this radiance.

Inflorescence

Any path you take is a path
                                        of milk, of salt,
the cold shadow of bluebell wood.

If you cling to anything here—
          an obsidian shard, a leaf of smutgrass,
it will be taken from you
                                        as dust.

This is where you end
and where you begin, where leaf-language,

earth's only divination,
          scatters through the wind's
                    fixed lexicon.

℘

I cannot speak for all the emptiness
          between the earth and me,

          the cold spaces that hold this clarity.

          To lie down in winter grass,
                    made hex, implacable.

          An omen branded,
                    burned through the imperishable meadow.

℘

Wasps seize the shed door then dip
to knotweed, cruel parabolas.

Demons squeezed into symbols
    to hum pain
    among the yard's stone coteries.

Yet the same gravities that lumber the sun,
    the moth, the word, drag them

down through spring rain
to thrash in clover, to amend
themselves to thunder in their paper hells.

Dogs bark at the sun-safe trees, where light
and shadow author act and meaning,

        green-heat and birdsong past all
praise and grief, motion, murder.

April carves through its brain again,
triggers its trillion ways to house a flower,

to sting and scorch with the fire
        of that cataclysmic star.

Spring Walk, Dusk

Out past the suburbs,
into kept land where
distance still sings hymns
called *clarity*, mind finds
itself bowered, grown to
language beyond tongue—
Cornflower sky and this
road's curve where wisteria
weighs down itself, spilled
to ground like blue-young
nebulae. Memory's blue
brain made solemn in galaxies
of pollen, sexed earth
sprung in moth-hoards,
moss. Stars strewn above
this spinning dark, all
leaves shrines of bluest
fire, vestige light.

The Milk Witch

Her head wrapped in torn red rags,
her fist clinched red around bail,
she edged down to the broken
waters of Moon Creek at dusk,
her tongue dry as winter stone,
sludged through the ice-shelved oxbows,

and came upon gooseberry
bushes not yet bloomed. She cast
a towel of soft silk twill
on their bare twigs and limbs, wrapped
them hidden like some mountain
Arachne, let the ends hang

down to brush the frigid loam.
Next she tucked the iron pail
beneath the shrouded hedge where
milk plashed, flowed, then spilled over
the pail's lip, voluminous.
Then she stole through night back up

to the dimming fire of her
shack, grinned toothless as dogs howled
the starlit valley alive,
some cold ember stoked bright-hot
in their brains, their sad language
lost to hill farmers' deep sleep.

That spring, those highland cows gave
no milk, their utters dry as
sleeves of droughted corn, and fields
in which they fell withered brown
and desiccate, the season's rain
locked behind her smiling eyes.

Jack, Snake-bitten, 1937

Came to in water. Alone.
Up in the late dusk loft-light
of the creek,

Jack bled out of the heath
of thistle and Virginia creeper

and walked the fern trail

(their carboniferous tongues scraping
sky and the gliding-past
of his haggard eyes),

itch of peach-fuzz in his palms,
sweat-salted on his neck's nape and drenched

in the sweet-noxious specter of fruit syrup
and pesticides,

went back to the water

and slocked into its slushy phonics,
his feet stirring

over one quintillion atoms

in each square inch of minnow,
silt, water grass, spider lily bulb

(emerald fist with the long leaves
flowed flat into forced prayer)

Stumbled into the field, homeward toward lantern pole,
careened into a vision without direct sight
of bones that stitched the loam under the orchard
trees he wove between. Poison unleaving.

Maybe I come a tornado
and wing through yonder
land and throw up all serpents
hisswise and tack them through lampposts

Well they'll be up in them limbs
stretched out like haughty vines
won't come down groundwise
eatin plums and they'll

He flowed chary as a snake—
slant as buried water that grafts blooms of pure dark,

just situate such that I can
glance their skulls clearlike
right through the blessed scales
and lattice rows, orchard brains

night-splay of primrose and jasmine that was not there
before his fever forced these false blooms' rapid growth
over the pine and pennywort that were

just coil up in their houses
and slip through their own souls
and make a Christ of their nest
and carry their blood-lit eyes

out to the trees to fake death
and then my hand and me'll
go down there to nail their square
heads to the ground with fire

His feet slapdash,
a play of flower-stain on stone, the world
behind his eyes turning on the tip
of a moon-cold fire, false equinox.

I ain't set right one way or other
up from the creek and the peach
smells gone rotten. Take my time
these clods on my boots sucking

my own air. Lung feet. On windy
nights the sparks will be thrown
high and the smoke will curdle them
stars to sour as my wife's milk, hair

Red earth reared up again. Hit.

Eight Essays on a North Carolina Farm, 1920

1.

First, peripheries:
the creek like a silver serpent
through stands of blue ash, poplar.
A lunar milk stilled in pools.
Flame-flash of minnows,
apple-red.

2.

The moon, a hidden coin
of dust, dims, sinks
deep through
the blue-tipped spring
of dawn.

3.

An apple on the sill,
chilled in the open winter air,
conceals its bitter core.
Outside, the tinct of leaf-fire,
blood.

4.

He walks around the shadow
of the shed and the sun
finds him and now
he is gone.

5.

Char of the grackle's song.
Walnuts, rimed
with rot, pock the grass, their smell
part basil, lemon, skunk.

Quartz points, knapped by hands
buried for centuries, shot through flesh
long melded with the spines
of earth, blossom-stems,

turn up
in land cannelured by rain.

6.

Somewhere west, hounds bay.
She shucks the corn,

snaps fat coinage of beans
into the basket of her lap,

rises, carries the yield
to boiling water.

Now the kitchen sings
in sluices, strained flour

and milk, the biscuits rolled
and buttered and fluffed, burbles

of okra and corn pone sizzle,
salty cuts of country ham.

7.

In the cellar bin, canned beans
and tomatoes, vinegar and oil,
land's bright vegetables

for years preserved

in loam-damp dark.

8.

Both of them old
before their time,

work-torn, blood still warm
through callous hearth, home.

The Farmer Who Loved Winter

He loved the killing frost that checked the sap,
that silenced the cicada's long debate. Even
springs and summers, when green

heaved him out to fields to work
from dark to dark, his small sleep bought
dreams of snow-cold ground,

dawn's December veil. Trains railed north
to colder countries, rolled from his county
through mountain towns till they hit taiga

yards, unpacked their frigid coal. And as he raked hay
from the barn's hot loft, his mind's slate of earth
was always bare, the fields gray, his wife's hair

spiced with conifer. When true winter
came, he walked his barren country, knew
darnel and thistle and naked wood were

merely stilled, the core pulsing its hidden life.
The axle of the moon was cleansed and sharp
in bitter air. Stars wheeled round the farm.

No harm to him: Their salt shimmer
slaked his mind to know the soul's residuum
long outglowed leaf or flesh, stem or stone,

returned to join and root in some new
flagrant spring, ghost-grown, abiding.

A Path of Walnut Trees after Rain

To be clothed in the smell,
a skin of sweet-rot, flowery,
life-dark as a pond floor—
their fruit felled, wet, fat,
half-black, half-green in slack grass
sugared in bees and calyx sap,
where blue squill and fern lift
to a bedraggled sun
from this pocked ground,
its mosses bright, this vanishing,
and later, starblown night.

Silence

Star-arc and cold April night,
distant truck-hum and dim growl

downshifting north to some small town
off-ramp, where stand

pines grown tall though never seen,
        even once, by any human eye.

        Aqueous, benefic under stars.

Now in their jags
        the body of a wren
        putrefies, the flesh eaten away by air,

riding wind.

        This chalice.
        This votive silence.

Ghosts in Winter

They're born from the attic's riven boards
of burned-down houses, or stints of sleet
that slant from the northeast gap of lightless
clouds, the capricious god that gives them
form: their skin a rime of frost, blue fires

that, if seen, disperse into the air quick
as vapor, rise in a silent roar back through
the frigid veins of their own making. Rush-rasp
tides leak their names, erase them swiftly
as they were voiced. For centuries, they've walked

beyond their lives to stall in pungent cores
of ice-pocked cedars, dark dapples
of snow-shadow under the shed's rusted roof,
or full moonlight that finds the sleeping
ears of their children's distant heirs,

a blood barely shared. Something like thirst,
like yearning, forever pulses in them
like heartbeats, the burl and salt of their mouths
yawning wide in the dark, then falling
again as ash to grass, earth's final word.

Nightfall

After two lines by Tomas Tranströmer

1.

Over the world goes a graver storm.
Bones sputter in the bone-smoke,
the fire coughing blue-hot
in this coldest twilight.

Twigs darken to a caul of ash.
At the edge of the wood the air is warm—
I gesture like a vine toward that dark,
then enter to gather rain-sagged wood
for kindling and feel the old ghosts
looking on.

Thunder barks down the distance—
clouds embrace, tear themselves apart.

I rub the fire back to a fluttering heart and see
the outline of your body where you have lain
and left, that dry, flat space gone
to the kingdom of grass.

2.
Last night, when I woke again
into a dream of winter, I smelled wood smoke
on the wind and saw someone sleepwalking
far out on the hill,

their hair blowing wildly as fire
without light.

They lost themselves
to the standing graves of corn,
vanished over the crest
into a valley of silent birds, where
dawn burned the trees alive.

3.
The hieroglyphs of evening: moon
filters through woods
and strikes the mossy floor with marrowlight,
sun's last comment.

Pines gossip,
rumor built from sounds of sea-tides,
whisper-snaps and collapses, then slow givings-in
to wind.

Language of sleep,
winter narcosis.

4.
In a small room of pungent cedar,
your body leans into mine.
Your eyes pierce like a star.

History of the Last Man

When language left him, in silence
he hauled kindling day after day
from the shardblue banks to fight
dusks drawn tight and cold
as skins of ice over his back.

Sleep: always a burning entrance
to the edge of dawn. Sleep: earth-slant
roiling with clouds over images
never recalled upon waking: fishbones
and fern, some genetic memory fatherwitted,

then snatched back when he rose
to move on, on under skies of ash
and fire, under the broken moon
screaming the tides riotous. He
knew not love, for his heart

was caulked in shadow. He knew
no music or offering, for his heart
turned in him knotted, nerveless,
hard and pineal as the skull of a snake.

Question

A black wolf followed me
through a snow-roofed wood.

We went on for miles through the limb
creaks, the windrows and wet-crisp

footfalls. Silences. I came to know
her heart—I came to know she carried it

in her mouth. She meant no harm.
We climbed a hill of trees for many hours.

Then, a clearing, a field of cabbage. Distance:
one lit window, one lantern.

Here she let me pet her withers,
her warmth. I watched her throat pulse

in that tiny light, her eyes emerald against
the field. That far ember: a fire,

the promise of bread. She turned back
into her wildness, the barren wood we'd left.

I watched her go. Tell me: How, in dream
and on waking, did I feel an absence

so complete that, just then,
I would have followed her into death?

A Study of Descent

Crabapple falls, flicked
by sun-strike and limb,
to patches of spaghnum
moss and twigs, right
into a cup of shale set slant—
then rolls, bruised,
to a bank of brown grass
where a creek speaks
its million silences.

WILLIAM WRIGHT is the author of seven collections of poetry: three other full-length books, including *Night Field Anecdote* (Louisiana Literature Press, 2011), *Bledsoe* (Texas Review Press, 2011), and *Dark Orchard* (Texas Review Press, 2005). Wright's chapbooks are *Sleep Paralysis*, Winner of the South Carolina Poetry Initiative Prize, selected by Kwame Dawes (Stepping Stones Press, 2012), *Xylem & Heartwood* (Finishing Line Press, 2013), and *The Ghost Narratives* (Finishing Line Press, 2008). Wright is Series Editor and Volume Co-editor of *The Southern Poetry Anthology*, a multivolume series celebrating contemporary writing of the American South, published by Texas Review Press. Additionally Wright serves as an assistant editor for *Shenandoah*, translates German poetry, and is editing three volumes, including *Hard Lines: Rough South Poetry* (The University of South Carolina Press, 2015) (with Daniel Cross Turner). Wright will serve as Writer-in-Residence at the University of Tennessee in spring 2016.